Granite's Voice

GRANITE'S VOICE

POEMS
OF NEW HAMPSHIRE

Philip Cate Huckins
with poems by Sarah Huckins

ISBN 978-0-9969719-9-7

These poems were originally published in the following
publications: *The Henniker Review:* "The Radish." *Northern New England Review:* "Spring Goats" and "The Last Nail." *The Cancer Poetry Project Anthology II:* "Hospice."

Booksmyth Press
Shelburne Falls, MA
www.thebooksmythpress.com
Cover photo: The Old Man of the Mountain, Franconia
Notch, New Hampshire, Vintage postcard circa 1900, public
domain digital image Cardcow.com.

Iron sharpens iron, so one person
sharpens another.   *Proverbs 27:17*

I would like to thank
all those who encouraged me and
all those who discouraged me
in the creation of this book.
Each of you contributed
in your own way.

List of Poems

GRANITE'S VOICE

Sarah Huckins

Black Velvet

This is a story about stories,
a story about stories
about people I never knew.
My family knits stories,
each generation purling stitches
until a new pattern is born.

Moses Cate is a family legend,
the epitome of New Hampshire grit.
It is said that one of his journal entries read:
"Broke leg in morning, hauled rocks in afternoon."

I never knew Moses Cate.
No one alive now ever knew Moses Cate.
No one to correct us as we wove our innocent lies,
quietly ignoring the fact that Moses really wrote:

"Broke road in morning, hauled logs in afternoon."
We still talk about Moses and his rocks
while my father and his brothers
drink cheap Canadian whiskey
in homage to Robert Huckins, my grandfather.

I never knew my grandfather either.
What I know is what I have been told,
shards of stories that don't make a whole.
He loved sunflowers and Stephen King novels.

My father and his brothers tell the same story
every Christmas,
of how Robert would take his glass of Black Velvet

and sit on the front porch blasting Christmas carols
until the electric motor on the turntable would freeze.
Silent Night was his favorite.

And even if it wasn't, it is now.
With these stories we place ourselves at a safe distance
and then burn the bridge between reality and truth.
We become nostalgic for a past that may never have
existed.

It's like my grandfather Robert always used to say,
"They don't make 'em like they used to,
but then they never did."

GRANITE'S VOICE

Philip Cate Huckins

PSITHURISM

I grew up in a small town,
a really small town.
It was an ordinary childhood,
almost.

From the time I was a small boy
until I left for the service,
and even after that,
my grandfather, my mother's father, Elmer,
lived about five hundred feet from us.

And in all that time he and I
never exchanged a word. Not one. Ever.
A wave as we drove by, sometimes,
but most often, disconnected looks.

My other grandfather died
when I was very young,
so I never knew what a grandfather
sounded like.

I would lie in my bed on hot summer nights
listening to the sound of wind in the trees
and the rustling of leaves
coming through the woods
that separated our two homes.

I would fall asleep wondering if
the soft, soothing psithurism was
my grandfather's voice,
calling out to me.

SPRING GOATS

In the fall of 1967 we found out Helen, our goat,
was pregnant.
It was just before the time to build a little pen
for her in the garage, the way we had in past years.
Father couldn't use the old markings
on the walls and on the floor.
This winter's pen had to have room
for what was coming, not just what was.

Near Christmas they came.
I don't remember if we knew and waited
and helped the way humans think
they need to help animals give birth,
or if the two babies were there one morning
when we went in to feed their mother.

They were black and chocolate brown,
which makes me wonder now if our other goat,
Clyde, had something to do with Helen's condition.
I wouldn't have wondered about it then.
I was seven.

The kids were very much in love with their mother.
They nursed constantly,
perhaps because they were hungry,
or perhaps because it was cold.
(It seems colder then than it is now.)
They stayed so close to her.
For comfort. For protection.
And because there wasn't really anywhere
else for them to go, the three of them
in a five by five pen.

Helen often looked over the side of the enclosure
with plaintive tired, rheumy eyes,
begging for a night away,
pleading for us to get a babysitter
so she could have some time to herself,
so she could have one minute alone
without a sharply toothed mouth digging
at her red and chafed udders.
But she managed. And then, in late March,
on the eastern side of the property
we had fenced in as a place for the goats
to graze and live like goats might,
we repaired a few holes in the wire.
We hammered a few boards on the goat house.
Replaced a few shingles. Put out the salt lick.
The water and grain buckets. The hay cradle.
(We still had Clyde. Where had he been all winter?)

On a mild Saturday, my father put a lead
around Helen's neck and coaxed her
out of the garage.
The kids followed to the edge
of the garage's concrete floor.
Their mother kept walking, but they stopped,
frozen, no doubt convinced that pre-Columbian
explorers and cartographers were right.
The world did have an end.
It was square.
If you kept going, past a certain point,
you'd fall off and just keep falling,
into an endless void.

But their mother knew better.
She smelled the molasses in the grain.
She felt the relief of an openness
that the winter pen had not afforded.
She saw the greening grass.
She also saw Clyde, and either to thank him
or to scold him she moved toward him, bleating.

But the kids weren't budging,
so she turned from the molasses, the green grass,
the open space, the healing teats, toward the
youngsters,
looked right at her off-spring, lowered her head
and said quite clearly, "Get out here this minute!"
Obediently they stepped off the edge of the
universe.

That's when it happened.

Think of all that you know.
The taste of peanut butter, the feeling of poison ivy,
colors, the smell of pie,
the sensation of stepping on a rusty nail,
Christmas morning, a new car, prom night, flowers,
birds, chocolate, having to pee really bad,
feeling your father's whiskered face,
a branch across your neck on a cold day,
swimming, driving fast, failing at math,
diarrhea, getting into college, your child being born,
music, snow,
everything you know,

that you came to know over
all the years you are old.
All of that, and more, happened to them in a trice.

The new goats that had never
smelled a smell or heard a sound, or seen
anything that hadn't come from them
or their mother, were suddenly bathed
in a world of sensation they had no skills
to cope with. Their heads flew back,
nostrils flared,
tongues flashed out of their mouths.

For many minutes they simply jumped
up and down and to the side,
often falling over,
as if jumping were somehow a reset button
that emptied their systems of all the untamed
unfamiliar, but they were refilled with the new
so fast that they were for a long time jumping,
falling, getting up, and even when they fell
they were subjected to jolt after jolt
of the electricity of new grass coursing
through their little bodies.

Even their hooves betrayed them,
as they had not hardened enough
to protect them from small sharp rocks,
ants, worms, or whatever they stepped or landed on.
Seizures. Fits. Never seen anything like it before or since.

And then it was over and the kids followed their mother
into their new world where Clyde (their father?)
smelled them, nuzzled them, a bit too hard a few times—
they fell over.
They ate some grass, tried the molasses grain,
which their mother tried to dissuade them from eating,
more for her.
They drank from the water bucket,
climbed the 2x6 to the roof of the goat house and
quite quickly looked like they had been there
all their lives, which in some ways,
they had.

Twelve Things About Small Town Life

You can dial a wrong number
(using only four digits)
and still be talking to someone you know.

Driveway visits.

You and your father had the same
fourth grade teacher.

When you go to the market the cashier tells
you to put back the mustard because you
bought some last time you were there
and you could not possibly
have used it up.

The Post Office is in Mr. Lindberg's
living room.

The policeman in town patrols with
his whole family in the car.

You can forget your wallet and still
leave a store with what you came for.

You don't lock your doors and if you do
the spare key is on a hook on the porch rail.

You walk home from school
to have lunch, by yourself.

There isn't a stop sign or traffic light
at any intersection.

People leave vegetables in your mailbox.

The town library is in your grandmother's
coat closet.

Home

A home is not a place.
A house is a place.
A home is a feeling.

A house you buy.
A house is wood, wires, windows,
paint, plaster, pipes,
mortgage, insurance,
tiles and tribulations.

A home you build, you give birth to.
A home has a pulse, a heart beat.
It breathes.
It has its own DNA
and fingerprints.
As it ages it develops funny smells
and acquires the same scars, experiences,
and secrets
that make you you and me me.

The marks on the door frame,
some from Dad recording the height
of each child at regular intervals,
some from the dogs scratching their initials
into the wood.

The blood stains in the carpet.
The broken and re-glued ceramic figurines
on the shelves, the casualties of
touch football games in the living room.

22

The dead pets buried in the field,
the hiding places in the attic,
the .22 caliber shell casings in between the
couch cushions, left there after shooting birds
out the sunroom window.

It is what we make it,
and thus it is us,
even if we stop living there,
even if we stop living.

PRETENDING

When he was young my father, Robert,
worked outside with heavy machinery.
He could move dirt around the yard
with a bulldozer
as deftly, as gracefully,
as a baker moves frosting around a cake
with a spatula.

There is no place I can go
to look at something I have built.

So when I can fix something I try to.
As long as failure won't make things worse.

I have tools, and know how to use them.
Even better, I know what they cannot do.
Perhaps better still,
I know what I cannot do with them.

But whenever I gather my tools
I hear a muffled laughter.
It is my Uncle Moses, or my grandfather, E. Guy.
They snicker. They mock.
They make me drop things.
They distract me so that I hit
my fingers with my hammer.

I have spent too much time away from dirt,
too much time in school,
to be taken seriously by these men.

Moses and E. Guy don't have time for
or patience with pretenders.
And I am a pretender,
not at home where I am,
not welcome where I came from.

Hospice

When my mother got the call from hospice
she declined their offer.
"If you can get here by this afternoon,
we can offer you a room."
Mom told them that she could not possibly
find a place for her cat that fast.
So, well, thank you, but no.

"Bring your cat," the woman said.
So, we packed a few bags and gathered up Barney
and set off for Concord.

We had known hospice was in our future
as soon as Dr. Hampton had said that the chemo
Mom was being treated with was not helping,
that even with that regimen of what was essentially
engine coolant being poured into her body
the CA-125 numbers were not coming down,
in fact, they were rising,
and this was Mom's third round of prescription poison.

So Dr. Hampton signed the papers saying that Mom had
the right number of months to live,
or die,
to be eligible for admission.

When we arrived we were given a tour.
It was a lovely place, really.
Kitchen, dining room, tv room,
overnight accommodations for family,
and a room to gather if the need arose.
Mom's room was bright, windows on two sides,

chairs, a bathroom, a closet, and, for Barney,
a box of kitty litter.

Each morning my mother was greeted by a
member of the staff or a volunteer who would ask
how she was doing and what they might
provide her so as to make her more at ease.
"Sarah, what would you like for lunch,
baked potato drowning in butter, with bacon,
topped with M&Ms?"
Mom would demur. "No. Not today."

It took Mom some time to get into
the rhythm of hospice,
but once she did, she went all in,
in her own way.
"Sarah, how can we brighten your day?"
Being a New Hampshire yankee,
she dryly offered,
"I miss my birds."

One of the staff members
heard what my mother,
the yankee, was saying.
The next morning there was a beautiful
bird feeder filled with thistle on one side
and black oil sunflower seed on the other.
Mom awakened to an explosion
of avian color and sounds.
That was Tuesday.
On Thursday a volunteer asked
the magic question,

"Sarah, how can we brighten your day?"
With the nearly deafening success
of her previous request ringing in her ears,
she tried her luck again.
"I miss my flowers."

The next morning she woke to
a vibrant, variegated garden
that had simply arisen,
much like color had suddenly
appeared to Dorothy
as she made her way to Oz.

With the feeder and the garden
the staff had made my mother
so much more alive
than she would have been
looking out the window
at the parking lot.

On a Friday, a few weeks later,
while my brothers and I
stood by her bed,
we began to hear
the death rattle,
so we knew
it would not be long.
At about ten in the morning
her last breath left her.

The birds were singing.
The flowers were blooming.

AMPSHIRE

People have all sorts of trinkets around the house.
Spoons, shot glasses, thimbles.
Something to jog the memory, to remind them
of what happened one day, a long time ago.

Early one Saturday morning in June of the year
that I was seven, my mother came up to our room
to tell us that the night before my father had
fallen asleep while driving and had crashed
head-on into an immense oak tree.

He lost his teeth.
He broke his right leg in eight places.
It was an inch shorter than the left
when it healed.
He smacked his head so hard
on the steering wheel that he damaged
his brain and had double vision
for the rest of his life.
He came home with a case of diabetes
that had probably gone undiagnosed
for years and may have caused the accident,
either that or he was drunk.

I have the license plate from the car
hanging from a hook in the cellar stairway.
It is mangled. There is a piece missing
from the lower left hand corner.
It no longer says NEW HAMPSHIRE,
just AMPSHIRE.

When my father came home
from the hospital
he was mangled too.

I don't keep the plate to remind me
of that day.
I keep the plate to help me wonder
what other pieces were missing.

It Is the Rope

In my house there is a picture
of the wooden bucket Moses Cate
used to draw water from the well
at the house in Brookfield.
It is sitting beside a coil of rope.

I have looked at that image
a dozen times a day,
and until today
I always thought the bucket
was the subject of the picture.
Then it dawned on me.

It is the rope,
the rope that is used to draw
the bucket back up
once it is filled with water.
A bucket in a well with no rope
is of no use to anyone.

That is what you are to me
and I am to you,
the rope to each other's bucket.

OKRA

My mother was a loving, caring woman.

She could sew, paint a picture, and knit,
but she was not much of a cook.
It wasn't her fault.
My father's gastronomic palette was
nearly monochromatic.
Mom cooked what Dad was willing to eat.

Dad was meat, potato, and one of a few
vegetables. Peas, corn, carrots, radishes.
But never, ever, could any of the
components touch each other on the plate.
And never, ever, a salad.

Not long after Dad died
Mom decided to branch out and try
new foods.
She went to Chinese and Vietnamese
restaurants in Boston with my brother.
She also tried Greek and Italian food.

She was doing well teaching her taste buds
new flavors and consistencies.
But she flew too close to the sun when
she bought a can of okra.

She had great plans.
She had experienced some foods
from far away and was ready
for the more locally exotic,
or so she thought.

Okra is, for a life-long New Englander,
an odd vegetable.
When cooked in some ways it becomes
slimy, sort of the consistency
of Elmer's glue.

She must have done some research
or perhaps heard by word of mouth
that okra was just too far out of her reach.
She put the can in the pantry and never
touched it again.

When we visited, Brad or Dave or I
would tease her about the can of okra
in the pantry.

Though after a while we noticed
that she did not find our jokes funny.
She would lower her gaze, put her chin
to her chest, and set herself to some
mindless task or change the subject
or both.

We stopped teasing her but we knew
the damage was done.

Now that I am older I have come to see
that we all have a can of okra in our pantry.

BEES AND SUNFLOWERS

I was cutting sunflowers the other day,
a housewarming present
for Jeanne and Amy.
Early fall, late evening, chilly,
sweater weather my mother
would have said.

Stuck in the heart of the flowers
there were bees, immobile.
They had stayed past their ability to leave
and would probably be there until
tomorrow, probably early forenoon.

A closer look brought a variant theory.
This was an embrace.
This was love.
Each had given to the other,
without regard for the consequences.

If bees and flowers can care,
then these bees and sunflowers
did not care.
The overnight cold could have killed
either or both.

If bees and sunflowers can be happy,
then these bees and sunflowers
would have happily died
in this eternal caress.

Nowhere to be other than
right where they were.

FLYING

I am feeling tired, worn to the nub tonight.
Not much has turned out the way I had hoped it would.

I am not ashamed to say
there is a tear in my eye.

I pray not with words to the Holy Spirit
but in recollections of my favorite dream.

The one where it is a windy day and I go
to the garage and get the plywood board
five feet long, three feet wide.

I stand it upright and lean against it.
I feel the wind pushing, lifting,
and we fly.
Effortlessly.

If I lean to the right,
we veer to the right,
over Parker Mountain.

If I lean to left,
we veer to the left,
over Bow Lake.

The birds don't know what to think,
much less the people looking up at us.

I miss that dream,
almost as much as I miss you.

What I'm From

If you are going to stay for the whole story
you will need a lunch and a flashlight.
This will take some time to tell.

The dumbest question anyone has ever
asked me is, "Where are you from?"
People who ask that question
don't really care
where I am from.
I could answer "New Hampshire,"
or "New Jersey," or "New Zealand,"
and get the same bovine response.

What they really want to ask is,
"Are you like me?" or
"Do we have anything in common?"

The question I want someone to ask is,
"What are you from?"

To save you the trouble,
this is what I am from.
(Take in some nourishment.
We have a ways to go yet.)

As the story goes,
and it may not even be my story,
but I have heard it and told it
so often that it is part of me now,
I had a great, great grand-something
named Moses Cate.

When Moses came down to breakfast
on the morning of his fiftieth
wedding anniversary he said to his wife,
"Helen, how has it been for you
these fifty years?"

Helen kept at her morning chores
as she replied,
"You have been a good husband Moses.
But I wish that just once in all the time
we have been married
that you had told me you loved me."

Moses, sat down at the table,
stuffed his napkin in the collar
of his shirt, and waited to be served
his poached eggs, bacon, and toast
as he had been for the last
eighteen thousand,
two hundred fifty mornings and said,
"My dear, on the day we married
I told you I loved you.
If things had changed,
I would have let you know."

That is what I am from.

Be on your way now.
Take whatever trash is yours with you.
Careful on your way home.

THE LAST NAIL

My mother and father
built the home in which I grew up.
It was a calming feeling knowing that
good enough wasn't good enough.

There was this funny thing
about the house though.
Just above the kitchen sink,
which was installed only after
measuring the height of my
mother's hips to ensure
maximum dish washing efficiency,
was one solitary finish nail,
in the scalloping of the trim,
driven in only half way.

That seemed odd to me,
given the care I knew they had taken
with every other detail of construction,
so I asked.

It turns out that while my mother
had been on the roof, nailing down
shingles, and my father was framing
and plastering, there were a few jobs
they had farmed out.
One of them was the trim.

Mr. Leavitt had been hired
to cut and to install all
of the finish work

throughout the house.
He was an older man, slow,
meticulous, his work the perfect
coda to mom and dad's
domestic symphony.

There was no hurry.
The house was livable.

One Friday afternoon
just as Mr. Leavitt
was about to pound in the
last nail, he stopped and put his
hammer in the leather sling
on his belt.

He told my mom and dad
that his arm and chest were sore
from all the lifting,
sawing, and hammering and that
he would drive and set that nail Monday
when he came to get his tools
and clean up.

While he slept that night
Mr. Leavitt's heart stopped pounding.

THE RADISH

The radish is the perfect, perfect,
New Hampshire vegetable.
As much a symbol as an edible,
it comes from the ground and smells
like the earth from which it comes.
Quietly powerful, it requires
no preparation.
It is durable.

Corn and peas and the other
above-grounders, they are
what the flatlanders prefer.
I see the weekenders at the market
buying vegetables trucked in from away,
from God-only-knows where.

They arrive driving new cars
with plates from Massachusetts,
New York, and a few from Vermont,
which surprises me.
These are the same people who buy
fire wood by the six stick bundle
for ten dollars.

Their basket is filled with box wine,
aged cheese, and French bread.
After they finish at the market
they drive the forty yards to
the grain store, where they try
to complete the transformation
from city to country.

Boots, flannel shirts, Carhartts,
maybe a John Deere hat, and always
the miniature can of Bag Balm. Always.
Then off to camp or cottage
to put away their purchases,
not a goddamn radish to be seen.

I Would Like To Go

I would like to go to your house and smell
the fire, your grandfather's pipe,
your mother's hands,
your father's wet wool sweater.

I would like to go to your house and hear
warm hellos, shrieks of surprised welcome,
laughs that must hurt,
dogs barking stories and news,
buzzers, phones, tv and the tink
tonk tonktink of ping
pong, and uneven footsteps coming
down sleeping steps.

I would like to go to your house and feel
your father's Sunday face against mine,
your mother's wet lips on my cheek,
your brother's double clasp handshake,
the embrace of a seemingly endless parade
of cousins in sweaters made by
another seemingly endless parade
of aunts and uncles, and
the worn finish of your
well used dining room table.

I would so much like to go
to your house.

The Day Irving Shot Clyde

One hot July morning Irving,
our neighbor, drove in the yard.

He knew no one was home.
I don't know how he knew,
that was before I knew what neighbor meant,
nor did I know where everyone was,
except that I am sure my father
was at his desk at Davidson Rubber
in Farmington, ciphering the company payroll.

I had probably hitch-hiked to Bow Lake
to swim for the day. Mother, brothers?
Not a clue.

Irving, being a hand on the Stiles farm,
had an abiding interest in husbandry.
He had just driven in to see how Clyde,
our goat, was faring in the heat.
Usually Irv would just drive in,
look through the slats in the wooden fence
at the end of the driveway,
and seeing all was well, would head back out.

Clyde, a routinized ruminant,
would always run from wherever he was
in his enclosure to the pen door
whenever he heard tires in the dirt driveway.

So when Clyde did not come clip-clopping
up the trail as he ordinarily would have,
Irv became concerned and dismounted

from his vehicle and went to the fence
and made a lot of noise, hoping to get the goat's
attention and have him show himself.

But Clyde did not appear.

Irv looked in the goat house and found Clyde,
lying on his side, taking shallow, labored breaths,
obviously struggling.

Irv retrieved the not well hidden spare key
to the house and went inside and called my father
at work and described what he had found.

My father, the son of eleven generations
of farmers and the first to work "inside"
as his father derisively referred to it,
asked Irving to stay by the phone while
he called the vet.

The vet said that it sounded like Clyde
didn't have long to live, and that the humane
thing to do would be to put the animal down.
The vet said he would be able to perform the
procedure. It would cost sixty dollars and could
not be done for several hours, and that if my father
had the will, he could do it himself.

My yankee frugal father had the motive,
but not the opportunity. So he called Irv back
and asked his friend if he had a gun and if
he would be willing to do what had to be done.

Irving said that he did and that he would.

Just as Irving was returning to our house,
having retrieved his .38, I was being dropped off
by the person I had thumbed a ride home
from the lake with.

When I saw the gun and the look on Irving's face
and noticed his determined march to the goat pen,
I began to worry. When he didn't bother to close
the door of the pen, I worried even more.

Our neighbor, our friend, took his gun and pointed
it at Clyde's head and pulled the trigger. So loud.

The bullet entered Clyde's skull just under
his right ear. I started to cry. From the underwater
vision of my tears I saw Clyde's eyes were still open,
looking curiously at Irving.

Then Clyde let forth a bleat, to ask why,
or to implore Irv to hurry up, to finish the job.
So my neighbor raised his gun again and
fired a shot that entered Clyde's head
adjacent to his first attempt.

Still Clyde's eyes were open. He let forth another
bleat and without hesitation Irving shot him
a third time.

The eyes closed. The labored breathing stopped.

Clyde's tongue went limp and oozed
out of his mouth.

Irving put the gun in his pocket, lowered his head,
went to the garage, got a shovel, and started digging.

THE VILLAGE SMELLS

I have traveled a bit,
Rome, Paris, Madrid, Reykjavik, Athens.
They all smell the same to me.

But, in my little hometown,
Center Strafford, I could find my way
about the village blindfolded.

A few yards from my house my nose
would be assaulted by the redolence
of the fetid water of the bordering swamp,
or the nauseating stench of
decaying cats in plastic bags,
drowned there by the neighbors
who had no room in the house
for the litter that had recently arrived.

Riding in a car with the windows down
I would know that we were passing the dairy
farm. On the eastern side would be
the acrid aroma of fermenting corn
in the trench silo,
on the western side, the bouquet
of the manure pile, either of which
would leave a day's long tang in my mouth.

Heading toward the mountain,
even the mildest breeze would
carry on it the intoxicating fragrance
of strawberries ripening in
George Thorne's fields.

At any turn an aroma unique to place,
the smells of the village,
an olfactory map.

TICKS

I live so carefully.
Don't smoke or drink.
Don't eat meat.
I obey the speed limit.
I exercise.
Don't take undue risk.

It isn't the Kenworth
that is going to get me
as I cross the street.
It won't be lightning
that strikes me dead.

It will be that little bug,
the tick, and all the little bugs that that bug
will put in me that will bring me down
when he buries his face in my fatty,
swampy, moist flesh and spews his
chronic disease inducing poison into me.

Once those little spirochetes are in me
they will dig in, like soldiers taking a beach head.
They are so smart, those little fuckers,
knowing when to retreat and to take cover
when the medicine comes to kill them.
They wait for the threat to pass,
emerging from hiding when it is safe.
Sure, a few will die, but those that remain
will be the smart ones, the strong ones.

I won't even know I am sick
until that venom begins to
throw my body out of whack.
I will feel like I have the flu.
My joints will ache and swell.
My memory will begin to fade.

Brought down by a killer the size
of a measle.
I should just surrender now.

A Bible in the Center of the Room

On Monday, August 28th of 1826
the Willey family,
all seven of them:
Samuel, 44,
Polly, 35,
Eliza Ann, 13,
Jeremiah L., 11,
Martha G., 9,
Elbridge G., 7, and
Sally, 4,
died after being caught
in a landslide in the mountains
up in Grafton County.

It appears to all who bothered to look
that the family, or some part of it,
was reading the Bible when they heard
the rumble of the rocks and mud and debris
coming down the mountain toward them.

Out the door they fled,
all seven of them,
and the two hired hands
who had come to help them escape,
were swallowed up by the mud.
Samuel and Polly, the hired hands,
and two of the children were spit back,
having been pretty badly stove up. Dead.
The other three children, never found.
The house was untouched by the liquefaction.
Still there as far as I know.

It outlived the Old Man.

A question has plagued me
since I first heard that story
and I don't know when that was.
Everything runs together now,
at my age.
Anyway, why did they abandon the house?
Some say to make a run for the stone shelter
not far away.
I am not convinced.

I want to know to what chapter, what verse
was that Bible turned.
Maybe the first chapter of Philippians,
the twenty first through the twenty third verses:
"For me, to live as Christ and to die is gain.
If I am going to live on in the body,
this will mean fruitful labor for me.
Yet what shall I choose. I do not know.
I am torn between the two:
I desire to depart and be with Christ,
which is better by far."

When they first heard the chaos above them
maybe they thought it was
the Lord
coming to take them home.
And so they ran,
not to escape,
but to be rescued.

My Moon

The other night
when I was driving to Concord
I pulled over to get a good look
at the moon, full, pendent.
Because I was so consumed by the moment
the State Police vehicle
that had crept up beside me
escaped my notice.

I think the trooper thought I was stoned.
I wasn't.
He asked, with simultaneous looks
of caution and concern on his face,
"Everything alright?"
Swooning, breathless,
a thin film of sweat on my forehead, I
replied, "Fine. Just looking at the moon."
I am confident that he would have been
happier if I had said I was too fucked up
to drive.

In a real but immeasurable way, I was.
The beauty of the moon had intoxicated me.
I had driven around the park and ride
eight times, looking for just the right
vantage point.

Once I found it,
I put the window down and twisted my neck
like a drain snake, looking for
just the right view.

This is not something sober people do.

One might say I have an obsession.
I always know where the moon is,
where it is when I cannot see it,
when it will return,
and the planets it is passing.

It is this kind of behavior
that gets noticed by the authorities.

FROGS

The music that transfixed my mother
was that produced by spring peepers,
little frogs,
little male frogs,
singing to attract a mate.

There were places along the route
to Rochester, Long Swamp comes to mind,
that had significant peeper populations.

In the evening, in early spring,
when she was traveling home from shopping,
Mom would drive slowly through these
amphibian neighborhoods,
windows rolled down, ears perked up.

I feared she would drive right off the road.
She never did. She seemed calmer after
hearing them. Less anxious,
at least for a while.

Mom is gone, but each spring I drive slowly
through those neighborhoods
and let the frogs sing to me.
They won't find a mate,
but they will help me find my way.

FARMS

When I was a boy
Center Strafford
had two dairy farms.
One was owned by Mr. Stiles,
the other by Mr. Pierce.

Mr. Stiles produced milk
for individual consumption,
Mr. Pierce for
commercial concerns.

Farming is a particularly
dangerous occupation.
You can look it up.
But, it was in the danger
that I found the excitement.
Sharp things. Heavy things.
Tall things. Horned things.
Motored things.

I drove my first truck at fourteen,
my first tractor at the same age.
I was a small child.
Some said wiry,
others said puny.

I knew how to operate all the machines.
It made sense that the smallest guy
would drive the tractor, not break his back
on the hay wagon wrestling bales into place.

But on the farm, as in the military,
shit rolls down hill,
and I was in the valley.

So I ended up on the wagon
working twelve hours a day,
lifting, throwing, packing bales.

Hay seed, snakes, sweat, lightning,
hunger, thirst, fatigue, pain,
nothing stopped the steady flow
of the bailer.

Nothing stops the farm
or the farmer.
The grass grows lushly.
The udders swell painfully.
The shit piles inexorably.

Mow it.
Milk it.
Move it.

Or work inside.

Charlotte and Grace (This is true.)

Grace and Charlotte, twin sisters,
had lived together in the same house
in Henniker for their whole lives.

For eighty-nine years they had
made that house almost their entire world,
coming down the hill from the Quaker district
once a year to attend town meeting.

And every year someone new
would ask the twins about their lives
in a small town.
And every year someone would say
something about the twins being
the oldest living natives of Henniker
because they didn't know that
on the way back from visiting
relatives their mother gave birth to
Charlotte on the Weare side of the town line,
and that a few minutes later, when the family
was in Henniker, Grace was born.

And when the question came,
as it always did,
Charlotte's chin would drop to her chest,
knowing that Grace was about to say,
with just a hint of scold,
"Well, my sister's local, but she's not native."

These Too Shall Pass

Each morning Edgar was dressed and out the door
in a single swoop,
perhaps to catch the cows unawares.
He never could.
All six of them would be waiting,
every morning,
for Edgar to open the barn doors.

If you put your hand in the gap
between the two sliders
you could feel their warm, damp breath.
Odd, the cows waiting impatiently
to be let in to the barn,
to be freed of the burdens
of being out
in the wide and free pasture.
Odd, the cows waiting to be confined
to small stalls
with their necks in stanchions.

There was a rhythm to this.
The cows loved the routine
as much as they were the routine,
it was a symbiosis,
a bovine Stockholm syndrome.
Edgar opened the doors and each cow
paraded to the same stall
she always went to and put her head
between the rails and Edgar obliged
each one by tightening the rails
tight enough so they could not escape
but not so tightly they could not breathe.

Grain for each,
a little extra for the pregnant one.
Hay and a quick check to be sure
that the water bowls worked.
They did.

Then a moment to look at them.
Just a moment. Lots to do on a farm.
Not a lot of spare time.
He gave them a quick check for cuts
or bites or runny eyes or infected teats.
All seemed in order so Edgar left the barn
and got in the truck and beeped the horn
to let Helen, Mrs. Hammersmith,
know it was time to go to town to get
grain and other sundries.

Not long after they had gotten underway,
just before the turn onto Morrison Road,
Edgar felt a bolt of pain in his stomach.
The kidney stones again.
"These too shall pass,"
Edgar muttered to himself.

They were not gone long.
They were not social.
They did not shop; they bought
what they needed that the exchange had.
They ordered what they needed
that the exchange did not have,
to be picked up
on the next trip to town.

Errands done, they headed back
to the farm.
Edgar, in his head, making a list of the chores
he would have to complete before bed.
Just as the truck crested the hillock
the farm came into view.
Edgar was jolted out of his bemused state
and what he saw paralyzed him, mind and body.
His head hit the steering wheel.
His dentures clattered to the floorboards.
The truck edged into the ditch the rain had dug.

Helen looked up and saw what Edgar had seen,
six cows hanging by the neck,
having fallen through the floor,
the joists having given way to age and weight.
Six cows, six swollen tongues,
six engorged udders, twelve open eyes
looking straight toward heaven.

MOM AND DAD, THE FIRST DAY OF FALL

My mother comes into the breakfast nook
dressed in her overalls. a white
honeycomb weave undershirt,
construction boots,
and her wide-brimmed blue hat.

My father, already at the table,
smiles as he sees her come in.
His breakfast is in front of him,
scrambled eggs, dry,
bacon, crispy, nearly dust.
English muffin, toasted,
butter filling each cranny.

Mom eats quickly. Oatmeal and Sanka.
Clears her dishes and his.
They head to the shed to gather
materials and tools.

Mom: paints, brushes, and cleaning rag,
but no drop cloth.
Dad: ladder, assorted tools, and wagon
to carry all of their hardware.

Off they go to the forest,
as they have each first day of fall
for a long time.
Dad puts his ladder against the trunk
of a maple tree and pulls on the rope
sending the extension
to the top of the tree and seats the feet
into the humus.

Mom, as sure-footed as any alpinist,
sprints up the rungs and disappears
into the canopy of leaves.

She steps out onto a branch
never hesitating, reminding me of
the pictures I have seen of iron workers
building sky-scrapers,
strolling along I-beams like
they were walking
down the boulevard.

She has her paints, yellows, golds, reds,
lots of reds, and browns, though
she hates using the browns.
She takes a brush and begins to slowly
cover the canvas of each green leaf
with a random offering of rich colors,
always the perfect mix of hues.

Skittering from branch to branch,
moving from top to bottom,
as good painters do,
she finishes more quickly
than she would have liked.

Time to get the next tree
ready for the season.
As she climbs down she calls to Dad,
who is sitting on the warm ground,

leaning against the ladder,
sleeping.

She smiles and sits beside Dad.
Closes her eyes.
No hurry.

Piss Oak

It isn't that people from New Hampshire
are smarter than flatlanders.
We just know more about important things.

My mother could tell the type of wood
being split and stacked outside her window
by the smell. She knew the piquant
minty aroma of grey birch and the foul smell
of what she called piss oak.

My father knew how to express his
feelings with clever sayings like,
"hard sayin', not knowin,"
"if it doesn't fit, get a bigger hammer,"
"you can put kittens in the oven,
doesn't make 'em muffins," and
"use it up, wear it out.
make it do, do without."

Everyone knows about wood and hardware,
that the only way to stack wood
is bark up, the dimensions
of a cord, the difference between
a rip saw and a crosscut saw,
what a kerf is, how to fell a tree, and
ten uses for an 8d nail that have nothing
to do with a hammer.

We know so much more about animals
than people from away.
We call cows beef creatures.

We know the difference between
Angus, Hereford, and Jersey,
how to hang an ox yoke,
why the taste of cheese and
milk change as the weather gets colder,
and why you should feed your goat
cigarette butts.

It's not that we are smarter,
it is just that we know more
about important things.

GRANITE'S VOICE

Sarah Huckins

Partners In Crime

My father's brothers used to shoot
at him with BB guns.
They pretended they didn't know him
at school.
They were older, thus infinitely cooler.

But the gap between them
narrowed with time.
Now they are bound by
the stories of their childhood.

Brothers who became friends,
partners in crime.
All three, witnesses to a time
that no longer exists.
They carefully curate the relics
that survived this age.

But one artifact
needed excavation.
After turning over the keys
to the new owners
of their mother's home,
they realized, too late,
what they had left behind.

The panel that cased the door
to the kitchen cabinet,
etched with ancient characters,
marking their heights and the
corresponding dates.

One night my father
entered the empty house,
and gently pried the panel
off the wall,
leaving a gaping hole.

He retreated to the garage,
where his father's tools
still hung from the walls
and cut a new panel,
staining it darker and darker.

For the last time
he entered the house
that was no longer his
and hammered the falsified panel
into its place.
The brothers slept easier that night,
knowing that they had saved
a piece of themselves.

Colophon

Poems and titling composed in
LTC Goudy Oldstyle Pro,
a classic old-style serif typeface
originally created by Frederic W. Goudy
for American Type Founders in 1915.
Its graceful design makes it
especially suitable for poetry.

mpliance